Down
& Dirty
The Secrets of Soil

Is All Soil the Same?

by Ellen Lawrence

Consultant:

Shawn W. Wallace
Department of Earth and Planetary Sciences
American Museum of Natural History, New York, New York

BEARPORT
PUBLISHING

New York, New York

Credits

Cover, © Sonpichit Salangsing/Shutterstock, © Jorg Hackemann/Shutterstock, © Ratikova/Shutterstock, and © Tatiana Belova/Shutterstock; 4, © IrinaK/Shutterstock; 5, © Alexander Raths/Shutterstock; 6, © meunierd/Shutterstock; 7, © Matt Jeppson/Shutterstock; 8, © michal812/Shutterstock, © vvoe/Shutterstock, © optimarc/Shutterstock, and © www.sandatlas.org/Shutterstock; 9, © NaughtyNut/Shutterstock, © Ilizia/Shutterstock, and © Imageman/Shutterstock; 10T, © David Lade/Shutterstock; 10B, © schankz/Shutterstock; 11, © Ozgur Coskun/Shutterstock; 12T, © JoHo/Shutterstock; 12B, © Marvin Dembinsky Photo Associates/Alamy; 13, © suronin/Shutterstock; 14T, © Dmitry Kalinovsky/Shutterstock; 14B, © Petar Paunchev/IstockPhoto; 15, © photogal/Shutterstock; 16, © George Burba/Shutterstock; 17, © Jorg Hackemann/Shutterstock; 18, © apiguide/Shutterstock; 19, © Photo Researchers/FLPA; 20, © John Warburton-Lee Photography/Alamy; 21, © Robert Harding World Imagery/Alamy; 22, © Ermolaev Alexander/Shutterstock; 23TL, © Boris Ryaposov/Shutterstock; 23TC, © Petar Paunchev/IstockPhoto; 23TR, © wavebreakmedia/Shutterstock; 23BL, © Olga Miltsova/Shutterstock; 23BC, © Romolo Tavani/Shutterstock; 23BR, © beboy/Shutterstock.

Publisher: Kenn Goin
Editor: Jessica Rudolph
Creative Director: Spencer Brinker
Design: Emma Randall
Photo Researcher: Ruby Tuesday Books Ltd

Library of Congress Cataloging-in-Publication Data

Lawrence, Ellen, 1967– author.
  Is all soil the same? / by Ellen Lawrence.
      pages cm. — (Down & dirty : the secrets of soil)
  Audience: Ages 7–12.
  Summary: "In this book, readers learn about the different types of soil."— Provided by publisher.
  Includes bibliographical references and index.
  ISBN 978-1-62724-836-5 (library binding : alk. paper) — ISBN 1-62724-836-6 (library binding : alk. paper)
  1. Soil science—Juvenile literature. 2. Soils—Classification—Juvenile literature. 3. Soil formation—Juvenile literature. I. Title.
  S591.3.L3824 2016
  631.4—dc23
                    2015017879

For more information, write to Bearport Publishing Company, Inc., 45 West 21st Street, Suite 3B, New York, New York 10010. Printed in the United States of America.

10 9 8 7 6 5 4 3 2 1

Contents

Let's Investigate Soil

What can be brown, moist, and soft, or yellow, dry, and rocky? Soil!

Earth is covered with a layer of soil—but the soil is not the same everywhere.

A garden may have dark brown, moist soil with bits of dead plants in it.

In a desert, the soil may be sandy and dry, with lots of pebbles.

There are many kinds of soil on Earth, and each one is different.

desert soil

4

Why doesn't all soil look the same?

Plants take in water and **nutrients** from soil with their roots. Without soil, most plants couldn't survive.

plant roots

garden soil

5

What's Soil Made Of?

The main ingredient in most soil is tiny grains of rock.

Where do the bits of rock come from?

When it rains, water trickles over mountains and large rocks and wears them away.

Dusty wind blowing over rocks can also wear them away.

Tiny bits of rock break off from the large rocks, fall to the ground, and become soil.

Tiny grains of rock break off from this rocky cliff.

On the ground, the grains of rock become soil.

A handful of soil may contain large and small pieces of rock. Some pieces are pebbles that are easy to see. Others are tiny grains that can only be seen with a **microscope.**

pebbles

Colorful Rocks

The pieces of rock in soil can be lots of different colors. Why?

Rocks are made of hard substances called **minerals**.

Most rocks are a mixture of several different minerals.

It's the minerals that make the different colors in rocks.

Some rocks contain metal. For example, bauxite rock contains aluminum. All metals, such as iron, copper, and aluminum, are minerals. Tiny grains of these metals can become part of the soil, too.

bauxite

minerals

Many Ingredients

Soil isn't only made from grains of rock.

When plants die, they rot and become part of the soil.

The bodies of dead animals, as well as animal poop, rot and mix in with the soil, too.

These substances, called organic matter, were once living or came from a living thing.

leaves, twigs, and fruit from an apple tree rot on the ground

rotting cow dung

Soil has two other ingredients—air and water. They collect in the tiny spaces in soil. Plants and animals that live in soil need this air and water to survive.

Where do you think the water in garden soil comes from?
(The answer is on page 24.)

Rusty Soil

There are many different kinds of soil around the world.

In some places, the soil is red.

The grains of rock in this soil contain the metal iron.

Over time, the iron rusts—just like the metal on an old bike or car.

It's the rusty iron that makes the soil so red.

rust on old cars

rusty, red soil

Soil with lots of organic matter is good at holding water. However, red soil has little organic matter. Rainwater soaks through the top layer to deep underground. This makes the soil on the surface very dry and dusty.

fields of red soil in China

Smooth, Sticky Soil

Many places have yellow, orange, or pale brown **clay** soil.

The grains of rock in this type of soil are super tiny.

This makes the soil feel smooth.

Clay soil can soak up lots of water.

When it does, the soil becomes soft and sticky.

A handful of smooth, sticky clay soil can easily be molded into shapes.

clay soil at a construction site

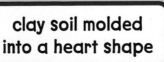

clay soil molded into a heart shape

adobe buildings in New Mexico

When clay soil is heated by the sun, the water it contains dries up. Then the soil becomes so hard it can be used as a building material. Adobe buildings are made from clay soil mixed with sand, straw, and water.

Soil from a Volcano

There are places around the world where the soil is gritty and black.

The ingredients that make up this kind of soil come from **volcanoes**!

When a volcano erupts, hot, liquid rock called lava pours over the land.

The lava cools, hardens, and becomes black rock.

Over time, rain and wind wear away the rock, and tiny grains of rock become soil.

volcanic soil in Hawaii

On the Spanish island of Lanzarote, the soil contains small black pebbles and ash that came from volcanoes. This soil contains nutrients that plants need to grow. Many farmers grow crops in the rich, black volcanic soil.

onion plants

volcanic soil in Lanzarote

Rain Forest Soil

The soil in a rain forest also has lots of nutrients. Why?

The ground in a rain forest has a thick layer of twigs and dead plants.

Over time, this plant material rots and becomes soil.

The dead plants become nutrients.

The many nutrients are why lots of plants grow in rain forests.

a rain forest in Thailand

rotting leaves and twigs on the ground in a rain forest

Millions of insects, snakes, birds, and other animals live in a rain forest. When these animals die, their bodies rot and become part of the soil, too. The animals' bodies also add nutrients to the soil.

Soil Is Special!

There's another type of soil that's made mostly of plants—peat.

Peat formed over millions of years from rotted plants in **bogs**.

People dig peat up and burn it for fuel.

This an example of one of the many uses people have found for soil.

Soil's most important use, however, is nurturing plants.

That makes soil very special!

a man digging up blocks of peat in Northern Ireland

Dead bodies, known as bog bodies, have been found in peat. The Tollund Man is a bog body that was found in Denmark. He lived more than 2,000 years ago. The peat had kept his body in good condition.

The Tollund Man is on display in a museum in Denmark.

21

Science Lab

Be a Soil Scientist

How many different types of soil are there in the area where you live? Let's investigate!

> **You will need:**
> - A spoon or spade
> - Small envelopes or plastic bags
> - A magnifying glass
> - A notebook and pencil

1. Look for different kinds of soil in places such as yards, parks, or forests.

2. Examine the soil right away. Or, collect a small scoop of soil using a spoon or spade, put the soil into an envelope or plastic bag, and then examine it at home with a magnifying glass.

3. In your notebook, draw a chart like the one on this page. Then record everything you observe about the soil.

4. Make sure you always wash your hands after touching soil.

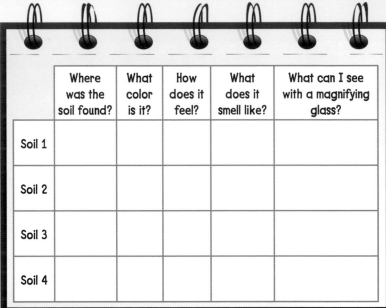

	Where was the soil found?	What color is it?	How does it feel?	What does it smell like?	What can I see with a magnifying glass?
Soil 1					
Soil 2					
Soil 3					
Soil 4					

Science Words

bogs (BOGZ) areas where the ground is very wet and spongy; the soil in a bog is mostly made of dead plants

clay (KLAY) a soil that is sticky and easily molded when wet and becomes hard when baked

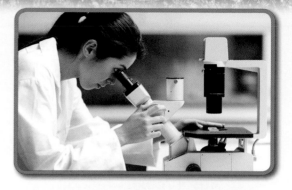

microscope (MYE-kruh-skohp) a tool used to see things that are too small to see with the eyes alone

minerals (MIN-ur-uhlz) the solid substances found in nature that make up rocks; quartz, feldspar, and iron are all minerals

nutrients (NOO-tree-uhnts) vitamins, minerals, and other substances needed by living things to grow and be healthy

volcanoes (vol-KAY-nohz) openings in Earth's crust that allow ash and hot, melted rock from deep inside Earth to reach the surface

Index

Read More

Cooper, Sharon Katz. *Using Soil (Exploring Earth's Resources).* Chicago: Heinemann Library (2007).

Lawrence, Ellen. *What Are Rocks Made Of? (Rock-ology).* New York: Bearport Publishing (2015).

Lindeen, Carol K. *Soil Basics (Nature Basics).* Mankato, MN: Capstone (2008).

Learn More Online

To learn more about different kinds of soil, visit
www.bearportpublishing.com/Down&Dirty

About the Author

Ellen Lawrence lives in the United Kingdom. Her favorite books to write are those about animals and nature. In fact, the first book Ellen bought for herself, when she was six years old, was the story of a gorilla named Patty Cake that was born in New York's Central Park Zoo.

Answer for Page 11

Rainwater and melted snow and ice trickle into garden soil. When people water plants with a hose or watering can, this water soaks into the soil, too.

24